# FARMER BROWN'S FIELD TRIP

WRITTEN BY
## MELODY CARLSON

ILLUSTRATED BY
## STEVE BJÖRKMAN

CROSSWAY BOOKS · WHEATON, ILLINOIS
A DIVISION OF GOOD NEWS PUBLISHERS

*Farmer Brown's Field Trip*
Text copyright © 2000 by Melody Carlson
Illustrations copyright © 2000 by Steve Björkman

Published by Crossway Books
a division of Good News Publishers
1300 Crescent Street
Wheaton, Illinois 60187

Art direction/design: Cindy Kiple

First printing 2000

Printed in the United States of America

ISBN 1-58134-142-3

LIBRARY OF CONGRESS CATALOGING-IN-PUBLICATION DATA

Carlson, Melody
   Farmer Brown's field trip / written by Melody Carlson; illustrated by Steve Björkman.
     p. cm.
   Summary: The Biblical parable of the sower who scatters seed on hard ground, rocky soil, in the weeds, and in good soil is presented in the story of a farmer who hurries to plant even though he has broken his glasses.
   ISBN 1-58134-142-3
   [1. Parables. 2. Stories in rhyme.] I. Björkman, Steve, ill. II. Title.

PZ8.3.C214 Far 2000
[E]--dc21
                                                            99-053086

| 09 | 08 | 07 | 06 | 05 | 04 | 03 | 02 | 01 | 00 |
|----|----|----|----|----|----|----|----|----|----|
| 15 | 14 | 13 | 12 | 11 | 10 | 9 | 8 | 7 | 6 | 5 | 4 | 3 | 2 | 1 |

To the McDonalds

Blessings on your family and farm!

*Melody*

For Howard, Roberta and David.

Thank you for the seeds you've sown.

You will never know how many

have fallen on fertile soil.

*Steve*

Old Farmer Brown smells spring in the air,

The sun shines bright, and he hasn't a care.

For Farmer Brown has all that he needs

A field to plant, and a bag of seeds.

He goes to the barn to feed his old mule,

Then fixes the seeder with a brand-new tool.

He mends the harness and checks the yoke—

Breaking down in the field is no small joke!

As he stops for a moment to pet his hound,

Farmer Brown's spectacles fall to the ground.

Old Molly the mule just happily munches.

Then down goes her hoof—Farmer Brown hears crunches!

Farmer Brown's glasses are broken for good,

And the poor old guy can't see as he should.

But he hasn't a single moment to waste.

It's planting time now, and he must make haste!

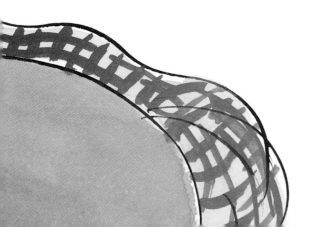

He straps the harness across Molly's back,

Then pours out the grain from the heavy sack

Into the bin that goes over the seeder.

He's all set to plant, and Molly is eager!

Old Molly the mule thinks it quite strange,

The way he leads her all over the range.

This certainly isn't their usual trek.

If this keeps up, the whole farm will be wrecked!

Missing the field, they plow down the road,

Where the dirt is hard-packed from its daily load.

But, nonetheless, the seeds are spread.

Farmer Brown doesn't see how the crows are fed.

Then beyond the road, to the rocky soil,

Where nothing will grow no matter the toil.

The seeding continues. The seed is tossed.

Poor Molly the mule is feeling quite lost!

After the rocks they go straight to the brambles

Where only weeds grow—an incredible shambles!

The going is tough with more seed to scatter.

Poor Molly heehaws: *Just what is the matter?*

Then at last they turn—almost by chance.

Into the good field, the old mule does prance,

Where seeding is easy—the soil is good!

Now seed can be planted the way that it should.

The rest of the day, how they plant and they sow

Till the sun sinks down, and the sky is aglow.

Then Farmer Brown stops and wipes off his brow.

"It's time to go home; we're all finished now."

*L*ater that week, Old Farmer Brown

Saddles his mule and rides off to town,

To get him a brand-new pair of specs.

Then back toward home old Molly mule treks.

H is glasses work great! He can see his whole farm,

But he stops at the road, crying out in alarm,

"Oh dear, gracious me! Why is all of my seed

Spread over the road for the birds to feed?"

*B*eyond the road old Farmer Brown walks,

Then blinks in surprise at the plants in the rocks

Where small, withered sprouts are baked in the sun.

"Oh, how did this happen? Oh, what have I done?"

Then he sees other plants choked by tall weeds.

"Oh, how in the world did I waste all those seeds?

Am I just getting old? Have I lost my mind?"

He adjusts his new specs. "I must have been blind!"

$B$ut at last the old farmer finds the *good* field,

Full of fine, healthy plants—a crop of great yield.

"Now this is the way I had meant to sow!

For it takes good soil for seeds to grow."

*"Behold, a sower went out to sow.*

*And as he sowed, some seed fell by the wayside;*

*and the birds came and devoured them.*

*Some fell on stony places, where they did not have much earth;*

*and they immediately sprang up because they had no depth of earth.*

*But when the sun was up they were scorched,*

*and because they had no root they withered away.*

*And some fell among thorns,*

*and the thorns sprang up and choked them.*

*But others fell on good ground and yielded a crop:*

*some a hundredfold, some sixty, some thirty.*

*He who has ears to hear, let him hear!"*

MATTHEW 13:3-9 (NKJV)